THE

HOPE

& BATTLE

For Our Kids' Future

A Parents' 7 Step Guide to Overcome the World

Joey LeTourneau

 INDEX

INDEX:

INTRODUCTION:

My wife and I are blessed to have eight children that range from twenty-seven years old to eight months old, and two amazing granddaughters so far. I've had the privilege to author over fifteen books now, for both adults and some for children. But I never planned on writing a book about parenting. Parenting is not a one-size-fits-all playlist. There are so many variables that don't have cookie-cutter answers to them. Every child and every parent are so unique, and on top of that there is not just one way forward either. That's why this is not truly a book on parenting. Though, it is a book for parents who want their family and their kids to be part of the solution for the world we live in today.

As a dad, and as a "Papa J," I'm growing and learning every single day. I'd be worried if I wasn't. So, while I won't give you "Seven Steps to Be the Best Parent", because that would be dishonest and frankly, incomplete. What we do want to give you are seven ways you can empower your kids to live out the full potential God created them for, and in doing so, become a generation free to shine their light and overcome the battles of the world.

Our kids are facing battles every day, seen and unseen. The enemy knows the potential of our children otherwise, they wouldn't be such a target. That's why it is so important that we as parents recognize not only how much we love and value our kids but realize who God created them to be and how powerful their light truly is. This small book is about us as parents taking our place in and preparing the way for our kids to be a generation that not only survives the darkness we're watching in the world, but to be a generation so full of light that they push back that darkness and take ground back from the enemy.

We offer you this book in hopes that we as parents can bind together to be the missing link between our kids, and the hope and future on the other side of the battle they're facing in the world today. God knows the plans He has for our kids, the plans to prosper them and not to harm them, plans for a hope and a future! (Jeremiah 29:11)

We as parents, have a big role in those plans, the most vital role. But to fulfill that immense calling as parents we have to see God's plans for our kids while yet surrendering our own. Remember that twinkle of light you saw in their eyes when you first met your child? Well, it's more powerful than you even know.

"This little light of mine, I'm going to let it shine. Let it shine, let it shine, let it shine!"

(Song originally by Zilphia Horton and/or Edward G. Ivins)

Thanks for taking this journey with us!

CHAPTER 1:

RECOGNIZE – The Arise & Shine Generation

As a parent, do you ever look at what's going on in the world and become concerned about your kids' future? Are you ever worried about the next insane political agenda that will be passed, with aim at your freedom and your say with your kids? But what if you had something in your hands to help "flip the script" and cause change in the right direction? What if your family isn't just something to protect but is a much bigger part of the answer?

The truth is, we as parents are the key or even missing link to seeing the next generation go from being the target to being the arrow. You as a parent, have the most influence on what direction the world will go over the next few decades. Not politics. Not schools. Not even churches. You! You hold the keys, and this book is purposefully focused to help recognize who God made your kids to be and how to take the next steps in empowering them to live that out.

There are two main things we must recognize. 1. The hope that God has put within each of our kids, and 2. The battle we are in over that hope in our children, which darkness would like to snuff out before it has a chance to shine.

We know the world—and evil—tries to wear parents like you down to the point where you're just trying to survive, and that sometimes leaves little energy, time or even patience for being able to give your kids what you truly want to give them. And honestly, that's their goal! The enemy knows that you as parents are the most threatening link in the way of evil's agenda. So, their goal is to distract, wear you down and make you stay on defense all the time, leaving no room to take ground back while you're busy trying to keep your family afloat in other ways. But that's not who you are as parents. And it's certainly not who your kids are either!

"He who owns the youth, owns the future."

Do you know who said that? The author of that quote had evil intentions when he spoke those words, but his strategy was spot on. And we can be reminded to use that same strategy in all the right ways. It is a statement worth fighting for, a statement and strategy worth flipping upside down from how he meant it and learning to maximize its truth for the full potential of good—and for the good of your kids and family. As parents, we have the right of first refusal when it comes to influencing our kids. We have first option at recognizing the investment they deserve, and the potential of that investment on the future. As parents, we can dictate where the future goes, but it will largely come down to how we see, value and empower the future that is right before our eyes.

The person who uttered that quote was Adolf Hitler. He was trying to wipe out an entire generation. But what will happen if we embrace the truth behind that statement to empower God's full, true light within a generation? Sorry, not what will happen if, but what will happen when we learn to see and empower that hope and light within our own kids, and therefore the generation that we as parents have already been entrusted with.

"...You are a chosen generation, a royal priesthood, a holy nation, His own special people, that you may proclaim the praises of Him who called you out of darkness into His marvelous light." (1 Peter 2:9)

There is plenty in the above passage to key in on. And each part has a place within the purpose of this book. But as we begin, my hope is that you as parents, see that phrase "chosen" and realize that it's not only speaking of your kids and the next generation, but of you as well. A generation can be a convergence of age groups that come together at one time in the world, and just as Jesus had John the Baptist go before and prepare the way for Him and His marvelous light, so do our kids have us to prepare the way for them to step into their "chosen" place. Simply put, our children won't likely walk in their "chosen" calling without us stepping into ours first. You as parents, have been given the ultimate privilege of empowering your kids to be who God created them to be.

This won't be your typical "parenting" book. It's more about seeing the light and the future that's already in your children. This is more of a "empower your kids to be who God actually created them to be" book. And if that's you, then welcome to the resistance. (I know, you were probably already there. But it sounds cooler and more "Hunger Games"-ish that way, right?) Speaking of Hunger Games, Katniss Everdeen's weapon of choice to overcome the enemy in the world was her bow and arrows. And what does the Bible say your kids are like? More on that soon though.

But truly, this is the other way forward. Jesus was revolutionary in that He always had an unlikely answer at the opportune time. And while we're looking to protect our kids from the big-bad world that's trying to huff and puff our family down, what if the very one's we might look to protect are actually the one's God is commissioning to be the light that will push back darkness? So, just like the song says, we can't hide those lights under a bushel, rather, we have to empower them SHINE!

LET THERE BE LIGHT:

In the beginning, God created the heavens and the earth. It says that the earth was dark, void and without form. But the Spirit of God hovered over that darkness, knowing the whole time the first thing He would speak to counter that darkness. "Then God said, 'Let there be light;' and there was light. And God saw the light, that it was good..."

I can only imagine the flash of light in your own eye when you first met your children. You don't fully know who you're missing out on until they are in your life. It's not just that they are a child, it's that they are your child, and who they are, the mix of God's image and the parents' family DNA is so unique that the world was void of it until that child of yours (each of them) came to be.

Is it any wonder that in those times around Moses and Jesus' birth that leaders possessed by the evil of the world sought to have so many children wiped out for fear of losing their power? Darkness is always afraid of losing its grip, and it has always been afraid of young, hopeful one's who possess the innate light to cast it out so naturally. Why do you think there is still such a battle for generations of children who have never gotten the privilege of seeing the light of day, or even more, how the world has never had the privilege of experiencing the light in them?

We all know the darkness I'm speaking of. It comes in many forms, but from one source. It's this darkness that has invaded so many parts of life and culture; schools, politics, media & entertainment, homes, churches and especially, now more than ever, identity. We'll discuss identity head-on later in the book, but for now, it's vital to recognize that when they're going after our kids' identity, offering such confusion in its place, what they're really going after is the unique image of God your kids are created in. Therefore, they're going after that light you first recognized in your kids, and it is the very place they so naturally shine from.

Darkness was there at creation. A void was there before your child filled it. And in Isaiah 60, we're reminded that darkness, even deep darkness will cover the earth, but in that passage there is a call that many are about to hear. And truly, that call is what this chapter and the book as a whole is here to help recognize. It's the call to arise and shine not because of the lack of darkness but right smack in the middle of it.

"Arise, shine;

For your light has come!

And the glory of the Lord is risen upon you.

For behold, the darkness shall cover the earth,

And deep darkness the people;

But the Lord will arise over you,

And His glory will be seen upon you."

(Isaiah 60:1-2)

Oftentimes, darkness becomes the usher that shows light to its seat of destiny. And during a time in the world where the darkness is becoming less and less hidden and more brazen than ever before, as much as we naturally want to duck and hide, or fight in more carnal kinds of ways, this present darkness may actually show us that we are primed for a fresh, radical light to emerge on the scene. Perhaps that light is right under our noses. And we, as parents, are the ones most called to raise that light up high and bright where it can truly shine.

"Behold, children are a heritage from the Lord,

The fruit of the womb is a reward,

Like arrows in the hand of a warrior,

So are the children of one's youth.

Happy is the man who has his quiver full of them.

They shall not be ashamed,

But shall speak with their enemies in the gate."

(Psalm 127:3-5)

I know many might wrestle with the idea of our kids being engaged in battle or warfare. But number 1. We're not necessarily talking about that kind of battle/warfare. And 2. They already are. They are engaged in this battle every single day at their schools, on their devices, with their friends, with games, movies and I can't believe how much my kids accidentally pick up just from watching what seems like a "harmless" commercial during what should be a "good" show. Our kids are already immersed in the battle, so we might as well empower them to operate and shine as they were created to. We're not asking them to go and take on things that they shouldn't, we're empowering them to BE the full, intentional, purposeful light that they were created to be and to know why!

Looking at the previous passage, our heritage is not meant to merely survive us and keep our family name alive, our heritage has far more meaning and purpose than that. Such becomes abundantly clear in that following picture the verse uses to describe our kids: "Like arrows in the hand of a warrior," and "happy is the man who has his quiver full of them." "They shall speak with their enemies in the gate." The Bible tells us that we will possess the gates of the enemy, a promise to both Abraham and Peter at different times. And here, we're told the impact that a full quiver has upon meeting our enemies in said gate. All that to say, the Bible is clear about our kids' purpose as we push back darkness and see God's kingdom established. Not only are our kids a part of it, but they are also essential. Just look at a few of these examples.

Samuel: At a time in the world when the "word of the Lord" was silent, when God was ready and looking for a voice to speak through, He called a young boy to be that light in the darkness. And do you know what the testimony of Samuel's life was despite his age and circumstances? "So Samuel grew, and the Lord was with him and let none of his words fall to the ground." (1 Samuel 3:19) It literally says that God "let none of his words fall to the ground." How is that even possible? With as many errant words as we adults can speak in a day, how is it possible that someone could be the voice for God starting at such a young age, and still shine in such an aligned way with God that not one word fell to the ground? It's because God was with him. God wants to be with our kids in that way too, in their own unique ways.

David: Most of us know the story of David and Goliath very well, but what is just as important is how Samuel, the same Samuel above, found David. David wasn't even brought in by his own father when told to line up his children to see who the Lord had chosen as the future king. David was young, and at the time he wasn't much more than "the other one in the field." But God knew what He had put within David. And God was with him, too.

It seems to me that the problem in empowering our kids isn't that they're young, it's that most of them don't know what kind of powerful light they have, and most don't know that God is truly with them to help them shine. Our kids may know that God is technically with them, but usually, and this goes for us parents too, we think of Him as "with us" mostly in a defensive or protective posture, protecting us from evil. That's true, but there's so much more! Or we are so familiar with that phrase "God with us" that we forget what it truly means. We forget to recognize or live into the reality that God is with us to lead us, to shine through us, to bring heaven to earth and to push back the gates of evil.

Last, but certainly not least, **Daniel:** Where was Daniel taken into captivity again? Oh yes, Babylon. Before he was in the Lion's Den, Daniel and his three (young) famous friends were captive in one of the most worldly, dark societies on earth. And what did God do with, and for Daniel? God not only protected him but used that place of darkness as that usher we mentioned before, the one that has a knack for showing light to its seat of destiny! Daniel was different, and that's why we love his story and example. But, was he really that different? Are your kids not created from the same image that Daniel was? Do they not have the same light, albeit their own unique one, ready to shine? What truly made Daniel different was that he went against the grain of culture, he did it with God, and he did it without compromise to the world and its ways. His light was alive enough that he had more effect on darkness than darkness had on him. Now that is what I want for my kids.

Do you want to know Daniel's secret sauce though? It's one of my favorites, and it really is so simple:

"...But the people who know their God will be strong, and carry out great exploits." (Daniel 11:32)

Daniel's light shone because he knew God, that's it, that was his part of the equation. And that is why it is so possible for our kids too. Notice that this isn't the kind of knowledge that you know about someone, but the knowing that comes from a relationship with someone. The simplest way to empower our kids, like Daniel, to be strong and to carry out great exploits in the world, is to be one of the people who know their God. We can't rely on other programs or people to do that for us. Our kids are watching us. Then they're listening to us. But they're watching us first, that way they know if the two match up. And if you know God, and they see the fruit of knowing God in your life, and then you take the time with them to introduce them to know Him for themselves, then, anything is possible!

I need to continue to do a better job of this myself. And each child is different, we have eight of them to prove it. But it's that knowing God for themselves at a young age that sharpens their arrow. Knowing Him for themselves will help them know who they truly are and start to see what the purpose is they were created for.

Daniel arose and shined in one of the darkest places, during one of the darkest times in the world. Such a destiny starts somewhere. The possibility of it began with the light in your own eyes when you laid sight on your amazing kiddos and the light in theirs. And from that moment, there is a battle for which direction that light will go. No matter how you have loved and led your kids up to this point, we just want to give you the opportunity to re-recognize who God sees your kids to be, who they are in your eyes, and how the best defense against the present darkness is a good offense.

Light inherently casts out darkness. Darkness can't cast out light, unless we hide it.

WHERE TO START:

- Pray Isaiah 60:1-2 over your children. Focus on them being part of that light that arises and shines.

- Recognize: What does that light look like in your child(ren)? Write down some of the unique characteristics of God's light that you've always, or recently seen.

- Talk with your kids about those like Daniel, Samuel and David, specifically looking together at how God used them while they were so young. Each of them knew God closely, and therefore God used them powerfully.

CHAPTER 2:

REVOLUTIONARY – Parent the Way

There are those people in the world that are just different. What kind of different can depend on interpretation, but often, God made them that way on purpose. They are often those that many of us might look at and go, "I'm glad I'm not that guy/woman." Or, those who we just brush off as being too weird and extreme. We tend to want those people to tone it down a little, and usually feel they should be a little more "balanced."

But is that always what God truly wants? Or does He want us to be revolutionary? What if balanced is actually just code for lukewarm? Or if they toned it down, would that rob that person, and rob God for that matter, of who He made them to be?

If there was a guy in your church community who lived in a camper in the woods, ate grasshoppers and chocolate, insisting on their protein value, always had this musky, no shower smell and look to him, and even said very politically incorrect things in the loudest way possible, would you look up to that person, or think they are more nutty than a Payday candy bar?

Now, you may have already figured out who I'm referencing in a roundabout way, so you're already thinking, "of course that guy would be welcome," all the while, we've probably all missed a number of toned-down versions of him in our time. Yes, John the Baptist was a little outside the box. Well, ok, waaaaaaaay outside the box. He didn't fit the box the Pharisees had built, and he wouldn't fit ours either. But do you remember what Jesus called him?

The greatest man ever born of woman.

And that's a direct quote.

You may not be called to be the revolutionary prophet, personality or voice of John the Baptist, but as parents, as crazy as it might sound, there are few better examples for us to emulate than The Voice Crying in the Wilderness—and he didn't even have kids!

John the Baptist never made it about himself, he prepared the way for Jesus, the Light of the World, always pointing towards Jesus and that light that God had in Him. That's why I can think of no better example (other than Jesus, of course) for us to remember as parents, and what that could mean for our kids. In a world that has so many of us as parents still pursuing our own success, promotion and self-worth, often at our children's expense, taking our kids along for the ride of those pursuits instead, what would happen if a whole generation of parents focused on preparing the way—parenting the way—for their kids to be the light that the world so desperately needs right now?

There's a reason Jesus called John the Baptist the greatest man ever born of woman, and it's because of the revolutionary heart and mindset he lived with, despite what it cost him. John the Baptist was counter-cultural in his approach (to say the least), and that revolutionary life led to the greatest Light this world has or will ever know. But I truly believe that we as parents have the opportunity to prepare the way for and empower that same Light to shine through our kids, individually and their generation as a whole. We have the privilege and the invitation to be the ones that parent the way for that arise and shine generation of Isaiah 60, and the chosen generation of 1 Peter 2:9—if we will step into the fullness of what we have been chosen for as parents.

You know who reminds me of John the Baptist? Mr. Rogers. I get that this may seem like just about the oddest comparison I could make. And yes, I understand that John wore garments from camel hair and Mr. Rogers wore sweaters and loafers; but stay with me for a minute. Mr. Rogers was revolutionary. He didn't have to eat locusts and honey to be revolutionary. He just had to be faithful at pointing away from himself and to the light that was arising in others. One of the most revolutionary things we can do as parents in the world as we know it today is to simply not make it about ourselves. And I'm speaking to myself here, too! We can't give our kids the leftovers and expect them to still live out the fullness of who God created them to be. They need us there consistently, patiently including them, sharing with them, constructively disciplining them, asking them questions, explaining the "why's," believing in them, loving them and speaking to the gold, the purpose, the LIGHT that we see inside them that is created to shine.

Mr. Rogers was there every day for multiple generations of kids, preparing the way for the possibility of their hope and future. In a world of busyness and more and more broken families, he was a revolutionary father figure. Mr. Rogers trained up generations of kids in the way they should go, preparing the way for them to have a chance to live something that they may or may not have been getting at home. He never made it about himself. He became successful, famous and influential, but only because he always made it about the kids and their families. He consistently empowered the next generation by pointing to kindness, truth, hope and consistency. Like John the Baptist, Mr. Rogers always pointed to the goodness and possibility in each child he spoke to.

FULFILLED:

So how do we do that? How do we parent like John the Baptist or speak to the next generation as patiently and selflessly as Mr. Rogers? I believe much of it comes down to where we as parents get our fulfillment.

In the New Testament, Jesus was constantly questioned about the law, all the while, he was ushering in something new, something greater. One time He responded, "I have not come to abolish the law, but to fulfill it."

Often, we as people become insecure about our place of belonging. We're trying to fit in, seeking to measure up, striving to earn value and worth. We're trying so hard, and often with the best intentions, to find our own fulfillment. And that's what makes it hard to fully point to and empower the next generation the way John the Baptist did with Jesus. We're worried about not measuring up to something. We tend to get our identity from what we do, rather than who we are. Thus, we get so busy in our "doing" that we may miss out on being "who" God made us to be as fathers and mothers, and the even greater possibility of being fulfilled by those we're preparing the way for: our children.

Jesus didn't come to abolish the old way, but to fulfill it through the new. And John the Baptist was the link between the old and the new. He was who the prophet Malachi spoke of in Malachi 4:5-6 when it says that one would come in the spirit of Elijah, turning the hearts of the fathers to the children, and the children to the fathers. John was the missing link between the old and the new. And the reality was, John recognized that he wasn't losing anything by pointing to the who was coming next, rather, he would be fulfilled by who was coming next.

That's how John the Baptist might parent. That's also our opportunity as parents. When we realize the revolutionary opportunity before us, not to be a generation of parents who are still trying to be fulfilled in our ways, but to be fulfilled by our children who come after us, we will set in line a domino effect of change and heritage we could have only dreamt of building on our own. In fact, that's the way God has always designed to build. But we'll cover that more specifically in the next chapter.

The reality is our ceiling shouldn't be our kids' ceiling. Rather, the simple but revolutionary life of it is when we truly live in a posture where our ceiling becomes our children's floor. Such thinking doesn't abolish us, it will fulfill us. That's why the passage in Psalm 127 says that children are a heritage from the Lord! Their lives build upon ours. They are part of generational wealth, and generational thinking. The kind by which we can also give the world the answer and the light it so desperately needs, by showing them Jesus through our kids. Think of a beautiful high rise apartment building in the city. Everyone wants the penthouse on the top floor, that's what is often reserved for the wealthiest. But our goal as parents should be to think beyond that kind of measurement. Instead of wanting the top floor, we should be honored when we help the next generation build their floor on top of ours. It doesn't abolish what makes us special and our part of the building. Why? Because their new floor, their new heights wouldn't be possible without building on top of ours. Our ceiling must become a solid foundation for them, and in doing so, the purpose of our place becomes fulfilled by the building of theirs. If we measure generationally, this becomes clear and natural. But the world has quietly, duped us into a "here and now" kind of measuring instead of generational perspective. This is the revolutionary way, the revolutionary thinking and measuring that we're taking back as parents. And when we do, we will set the stage for Jesus and His light to arise and shine through a generation when the world might be at its darkest.

Perhaps my favorite illustration in the Bible about what God has stored up in our kids comes from Mark 10:13-14:

"Then they brought little children to Him, that He might touch them; but the disciples rebuked those who brought them. But when Jesus saw it, He was greatly displeased and said to them: 'Let the little children come to Me, and do not forbid them; for of such is the kingdom of God.'"

Where do we even start? I don't know about you, but when I hear this story, it's easy to automatically assume that it was the religious leaders who pushed the children to the side. And we might chalk it up to the typical response we see from the Pharisees throughout so much of the gospels. But it wasn't the religious leaders. It was the disciples who pushed the kids to the side. Literally, the closest followers of Jesus were basically saying, "umm, not right now, we're busy with our more important adult agenda. Sorry. You wouldn't understand." And Jesus was not too happy with them about it either. That one really pressed Jesus' buttons as it says He was "greatly displeased." And then what did He do? He picked up the kids into His lap, laid His hands on them and blessed them. It wasn't some casual sneeze-level blessing either, rather, when Jesus put His hand on them to bless them, He said, "of such is the kingdom."

Jesus gave us one of the biggest clues we could ever need in order to see the Lord's prayer fulfilled. You might know that model prayer well, you know the one that says "Your kingdom come..." So, if Jesus wants us to pray for the kingdom to come, and Jesus says about a child, "for of such is the kingdom," then perhaps our answer is right in front of us, no? The kingdom of God that we so desperately need to see established on earth, the one answer we have to push back the darkness of the time, is found in the kids—our kids! You would think we'd put two and two together as believers and put all our time into discovering the kingdom in the kids around us, and then helping that kingdom light shine into the world. But we don't. We build more and more ministries (albeit many great ones though!) that fit our own grown-up agenda when the best answer might be the one hidden in plain sight and already in our care.

If the closest followers of Jesus automatically leaned the direction of prioritizing their adult purposes more than what was in the kids and didn't know Jesus' priority there, then how easy is it for us to do that? I'm sure we're all guilty of it at some point, if not more often than we care to admit. But it doesn't have to stay that way. That's really the whole purpose of this book. How do we transition from simply raising our kids—or in some cases, letting the world raise them—to empowering them and the kingdom purpose they so innately carry inside them? And then, we have a decision to make.

Imagine that scene in Mark 10:14 with me again. Which part are we going to play in that scene? Are we going to be more like the disciples, who want to focus on their adult ways of thinking, or are we going to be like Jesus, who sees what is inside the kids and blesses them for what He sees the Father put inside them? That choice might very well set the direction of our kids' futures and the future of the next generation in the world as a whole!

SO, WHERE DO WE START?

Probably the most famous verse in the Bible about parenting, other than honor your father and mother (we parents usually like to claim that one), is: "Train up a child in the way they should go, and they will not depart from it." (Proverbs 22:6)

I've consistently heard a statistic over the years from a study about youth who leave home and go to college. Sadly, the study found that 80% of Christian youth, when they leave home for college, also leave the church. As sad as that is, the more I prayed about the answer to that statistic I realized something. It's right there in the wording. It says 80% leave the church. Notice it doesn't say they leave God. I would venture to say that, unfortunately, many of those 80% never knew, or barely knew God personally for themselves. Perhaps they only knew the church. And maybe that's why they left the church?

We might take our children to church for eighteen years, only for them to leave the church. But the real question for us each day is, do we take them directly to God? I would guess that most of those 80% would never leave God if they really knew Him that well for themselves. It's harder to leave someone when that Someone is not a place, or an institution. It's hard to leave someone when you're walking with Them the way Daniel or David did, or, when you're keenly aware that the God of the Universe is walking with you in that way, too.

Are we raising up our children to know Him in that way? Like that promise in Daniel 11:32: "the people who know their God shall be strong, and carry out great exploits"? That is where their purpose begins. Because for our kids to start uncovering and walking in all that kingdom that's inside them, we must purposefully and intentionally take them back to the Source where such came from. God knows what our kids need better than we do. Even in our best as parents, we still only see a glimpse of our kids compared to what God sees. The light that flashed in our eyes when we first laid eyes on our children began with the light that He saw in them when He created them. We can be the best parent in the world, making every effort to teach, guide and lead our kids. They will gain so much from that. But sometimes even our best intentions can be a limit on God's best for their lives. It's important to learn to surrender our kids back to that Source of knowing Him. That's the best way we can prepare the way for them. Not by paving a successful road for them but daily creating a path back to the Source while reminding them that God has a special plan for their life.

The following is one of my favorite devotions from the book, Streams in the Desert, shared for the date March 29. Every time I think of this story it challenges my parenting and surrender further.

"Many years ago, there was a monk who needed olive oil, so he planted an olive tree sapling. After he finished planting it, he prayed, 'Lord, my tree needs rain so its tender roots may drink and grow. Send gentle showers.' And the Lord sent gentle showers. Then the monk prayed, 'Lord, my tree needs sun. Please send it sun.' And the sun shone, gilding the once-dripping clouds. 'Now send frost, dear Lord, to strengthen its branches,' cried the monk. And soon the little tree was covered in sparkling frost, but by evening it had died.

Then the monk sought out a brother monk in his cell and told him of his strange experience. After hearing the story, the other monk said, 'I also have a little tree. See how it is thriving! But I entrust my tree to its God. He who made it knows better than a man like me what it needs. I gave God no constraints or conditions, except to pray, Lord, send what it needs—whether that be a storm or sunshine, wind, rain, or frost. You made it, and you know best what it needs.'"

When we start to look at empowering our kids to fully be who God created them to be, it starts with acknowledging that He knows better than we do. Our kids each carry something different from one another, and they carry something different than us, too! Our best intentions can only lead our kids so far, and the only way to lead them further, beyond our best intentions, is to lead them to knowing God intimately for themselves, where they can learn from God Himself what He wrote into their lives, and learn to trust the Author, like David, Daniel and Samuel did, to be with them along the way—the whole way!

Surrendering our kids back to the Lord and His purposes might just be one of the most revolutionary things we can do. And hey, at least it doesn't involve us eating locusts and honey. But it does allow us to prepare the way for our kids to walk in the Light they were created for.

WHERE TO START:

- Pray about what it might mean for you to "prepare the way" for your child(ren). How have you done so already? How can you do so even more?

- Revolutionary: How can or should your family be revolutionary compared to the status quo expectations of the world?

- Take Daniel 11:32 to the bank. Spend time seeking God in prayer and worship with your child(ren) with faith that they will know Him more, and therefore will be strong and carry out great exploits from knowing God in that way.

CHAPTER 3:

REFORM – The Family Structure

It's natural, without even realizing it, to automatically think that our thoughts and perspective are the highest form of such; because for us, they are. At least for the moment. We assume we know best from our experience, acknowledging that our experience is limited but not necessarily that our understanding is. Even Peter, one of the closest followers of Jesus, questioned Jesus in Matthew 16:21-23, thinking that he knew the right way for our Lord, then Jesus rebuked him and said, "Get behind me Satan...for you are not mindful of the things of God, but the things of men." Whew, talk about harsh. But it probably also shows us how easy it is for us to assume, even when talking to Jesus, that we know best. Of course, we're not trying to do this, and neither was Peter, but we naturally do.

So, how much might we be missing out on?

The reality is, God does things so much differently than we do them. He has different strategy, different process, a much higher perspective, and a way different value system of measuring results. And we can be so thankful for that! This is why reform is so necessary. But, before reform can start in the world all around us, we first have to let that reform begin in our own mind and perspective.

While we usually build something according to the fruit we plan to see within our timing, God, in His much bigger picture, uses somewhat of a "heritage strategy," as we mentioned previously from Psalm 127 about the "house that God is building" and "children being a heritage from the Lord." Going all the way back to the Garden of Eden, God has been building differently than we might expect. And this is exactly why it's so important to realize how important our children are to His purposes and the ways He is building through us. Going back to David is the best place to start...

Famously, David wanted to build God a house. Like, really wanted to build God a house. He wanted a temple for God to dwell in, a place of worship and ministering to the Lord, something to catch the fresh move of God. On top of that, David really did have all the best motives and intentions. But in 2 Samuel 7:11, God sent the prophet Nathan to David with an answer to those desires...

"...the Lord tells you that He will make you a house."

What I find really cool here is that the word house has two different meanings. 1. It means building, temple, or physical structure. But 2. It means heritage, clan, or family structure.

So, really what you have is David wanting to build God a physical structure of a house. And God telling David, "No, I will make you into a family structure type of house."

Usually, we are like David. We want to build things for God. We build Him churches, organizations, and many kinds of religious boxes. I've built plenty of these myself. We are always trying to build God a physical structure for Him to dwell within, or to do His new thing within. But the truth is, if you go back to the beginning of time, God has always been building a family structure. And it's not that we usually disagree with that, it's just that for us the physical structure usually becomes the major and the family structure gets relegated to the minor. But for God, it's the other way around. We can see it for ourselves if we go back and look at how God moved and built in so many circumstances, as it was almost always in the context of family and the multiplication that comes through family.

In the Garden of Eden, God told Adam and Eve to be fruitful and multiply as part of taking dominion over the earth.

At the height of evil, God used one family, the family of Noah, to redeem mankind as everything and everyone suffered destruction from the flood.

When God re-started His purpose, He used Abraham as a "father of many nations", who would have as many children as the "stars in the sky and the sand on the seashore."

When God set forth the first form of institution among His people, the 12 Tribes of Israel, they were built through the 12 sons of Jacob.

When God gave His family lineage plan a jolt in the right direction, He used a kinsman "family" redeemer in Boaz to redeem a hurting and broken off relative, Ruth.

Boaz and Ruth had a son named Obed.

Obed had a son named Jesse.

Jesse had a son named David, who wanted to build God a physical structure kind of house.

But God wanted to keep going in His current movement and use David to continue establishing His family structure type of house, and through such birth, the line of Christ! Jesus, the Son of God and the Son of Man, gave His life so we could be redeemed back into the family as sons and daughters.

After He conquered death and was resurrected, He ascended into heaven and sent us His Holy Spirit, also known as the Spirit of Adoption. Romans 8 reminds us that "as many as are led by the Spirit of God, these are the children of God."

God has always been building through family. That has been His primary structure since the beginning. And though we usually have the best intentions, we are almost always trying to build like David sought to, wanting God to work through our more seen, tangible, physical structures.

Family has been God's offensive plan for thousands of years, and that doesn't change now. However, like God gave to David through Nathan, there is an invitation for us to adjust and learn how to fully join Him in building through the strategy of family. It's a timeless strategy that doesn't need reform. But if we will reform our thinking, our ways and strategy of how we build, I believe we'll see a generation of our kids and beyond become who God always planned for them to be!

A PARENT'S SECRET BUILDING BLOCK:

As it is with our kids, building God's family structure requires a special patience. That patience is key in any true reform. This is quite the opposite to the world's pressing influence for immediate gratification, which wars against God's strategy of big-picture heritage building. It reminds me of the counter-cultural choice we have between an apple and a seed. Most of the time, when offered to choose between these things, we want the fully ready, tangible apple. We can eat it right away and throw away the core as we move on to the next. It takes vision and patience to choose the seed. You need to have vision or faith for the tree already inside that seed and patience to see it through. Because on that tree are many branches. On those branches are many more apples. And in those apples, within the core that we typically throw to the wayside, are even more seeds that contain a generation's worth more of similar trees and yes, a lot more apples.

Patience isn't easy though, especially amid the world we live in. It's not easy in those stress-from-all-sides moments with our kids, and it's not easy to wait for results in what we are building that we can't "yet" see. This next verse gets me though. It's such a reminder that patience isn't a nuisance, but a powerful tool that yields many of the answers we're looking for.

"Let patience have its perfect work, that you may be perfect and complete, lacking nothing." (James 1:4)

Patience empowers process, and process leads to wholeness and completeness. To win the battle over the hope for our kids' future, we must reform our choice between that apple and seed and play the long game that God is playing. That's how we'll see true reform in their generation and in generations beyond; but it starts with our "now" kind of choices. Those choices must be made with both faith and patience, in mind. A lot of us have faith for our children's future and purpose. And many have patience to watch them grow up and wait and hope all turns out well. But too few of us utilize both faith and patience at the same time. Because when we use our faith to believe for something, we often expect it to be yield fruit quickly. And when we are willing to wait patiently, it is challenging to do so while still keeping our faith on and burning hot. There is a tension between faith and patience that is best revealed by the kingdom of God. And there is a true inheritance, even a family inheritance, waiting for us when and if we will actively apply both together.

"...But imitate those who through faith and patience inherit the promises." (Hebrews 6:12)

There is a huge lineage of promises God is waiting to bring about, and that family tree that He has always been building has deep roots and far-reaching fruit—we just have to see it enough now by faith in order to patiently wait and believe it to its fulfillment. As John 15:5 says so well, "I am the vine, you are the branches. He who abides in Me, and I in him, bears much fruit; for without Me you can do nothing."

UPSIDE DOWN:

Much has been said and written over the years about Jesus' upside-down kingdom, and for good reason. Once again, it's a picture of how much differently God builds. Our world and almost all our society's in-between are built upon top-down power structures where power and money feeds to the top, and then influence trickles down from there depending on how much the one(s) at the top want to relinquish.

But empowerment is about learning to give power away. It's how we build from the bottom-up. It's how God built through Jesus when He was born in a manger, and it is how Jesus empowered the disciples from the rough-around-the-edges, weary fishermen they were to the fishers of men that walked in His authority that they became. From moment one when Jesus called them, He already called them fishers of men even before they were close to being such. Jesus always lived His words that the last shall be made first, and He demonstrated through His ministry what Paul later taught that it's the foolish things that confound the wise and the weak that confound the strong. All of those are upside-down compared to the power structures of the world and are part of a grassroots move of empowerment that are possible from the roots of God's family tree.

Too often, our kids are taught the best paths of life are ladders of success that scale that power structure to somewhere near the top, where they will gain money and influence to create security and comfort for themselves and their families. However, God's upside-down building isn't hierarchal in nature, and its wealth is generational more than just monetary. It's a place where the least of these are meant to thrive, where power isn't kept but given away for the sake of building. It's a place where the meek, the poor in spirit and the peacemakers are promised the world as children of God. It's the place where Jesus sees other disciples pushing away the kids so they can make their way to the top, but He grabs them, blesses them and says, "This, here, them...for of such is the kingdom of God!" Jesus not only blesses the children but calls us adults back to such childlike ways and methods. Now that is reform in the purest sense, and it is completely upside down from how the world operates. Which is why we as parents must be so leery of getting caught up in building our homes and families in the typical ways. It's amazing how quickly and easily it sucks us in, and before we know it, we're trying to live by kingdom principles but within the world's systems and structures.

That's why we've written this, though. It is a reminder of how the internal reform in our perspective as parents can and will actually lead to the reform we hope to see with our kids—the kind that's being fought over by the world and darkness. If the world can keep us climbing its ladders and eating its apples, we won't use our influence to empower our kids while they're still young, from the bottom, and teach them these counter-intuitive, family structure ways of building that God has been using since the beginning. Our kids are full of that natural, God-given light that is just waiting to influence the world, and they don't have to be on top to use it. They just need to be seen and empowered right where they are. And we're the ones to see them and empower them before the world does. Then their light will be seen by the world in their true, God-given purpose like that awesome Isaiah 60 moment the Bible describes so powerfully.

UNLIKELY CATALYSTS:

There is a movie that helped me better understand the change our kids can bring when we, as parents, use our belief to make room for them in such a purposeful way. It's called Finding Neverland and is based on the story of James Barrie, the writer of Peter Pan. In the movie, James was a very established and successful playwright that had suddenly hit a rut with a few less than stellar reviews. The proprietor of the theatre was looking to him to create a new, big production, but James was stuck. Until that is, he found his footing while starting to hang out with a widow and her three children. That's when a whole new world began to come alive for him once again.

As James played with the kids and got back on their level, he started to dream and imagine with them a new world called Neverland. Before he knew it, the story and characters for Peter Pan began to unfold before his eyes. He wrote it up and took it back to the proprietor of the theatre, hoping he, too, would see the vision as their next big hit. But the proprietor couldn't see it yet. He essentially asked James, "what self-respecting doctor, lawyer or businessman from high society London is going to watch a play about pirates and fairies, Natives and fairy dust?"

James pondered the question and in so many words, responded: "You're right. So, on opening night, I want you to do this for me. I want you to save me twenty-five seats that are scattered throughout the auditorium."

"Who are in those seats, James? Are they paid for?"

"Don't worry," James assured him. "Just save me twenty-five seats."

Opening night finally rolled around and you could still see and feel the skepticism among those involved. The play was about to start, and those twenty-five seats still sat empty among a theatre of London's high society, all dressed for the occasion in their gowns and tuxedos.

But just before curtain call, James' surprise arrived at the theatre. Twenty-five orphans lined up to fill their seats. The children were a stark contrast to the other patrons of Peter Pan's first night, both in age and in attire. Still, James sent them all to their seats scattered among the adults. The play began and just as they predicted, the adults couldn't get it. They didn't have the eyes to see such wonder come to life. But the kids got it. They laughed and giggled. They enjoyed the peculiarities of the characters and story, the impossible wonders that defied worldly reality. And oh, did they enjoy seeing it come to life!

Before you knew it, the adults took notice of the kids who were engulfed in the story. And one by one, these members of high society in London came down from their perches and let themselves become kids again. They slowly emptied themselves of their grown-up ways at the influence of seeing the kids go somewhere that they had not yet been able to go. Truly, these twenty-five children led the way. From the bottom up, they influenced the adults to the point where the adults had found their inner kingdom again and were laughing and enjoying freely. The play ended with a rousing, standing ovation from both adults and children, a group that came together that night outside their typical societal roles, long enough to see the unseen world of Peter Pan come to life before them all. And it was the children who led them.

As you know, Peter Pan has become one of the most well-known stories in history. But it wasn't because the adults understood it at first. It was because they watched what was happening in the kid around them and followed them to a new place they couldn't—and wouldn't—have gone on their own.

That was the beginning of Peter Pan. And it just might be a picture of the beginning of ours and our kids' kingdom story as well.

WHERE TO START:

- Pray about what kind of "house" you want your family to build most, a physical structure or a family structure, and begin to pray it forward. Your prayers will help you focus on which one you will build.

- Reform: Think about which ways and perspectives you and your family want to reform your thinking in order to measure and believe the way God does.

- What is one new way you can start to believe in your child(ren)?

CHAPTER 4:

REDEEM – Your Children are Creative Geniuses

One of the most encouraging and hopeful things I have found the past several years in regard to the potential of our kids and their generation is from a study that was written about in the book Breakpoint & Beyond, by George Land and Beth Jarman. In the study, they offered a test that determines "creative genius" in individuals and began by testing young children, and then later working their way up to adults. The findings were revolutionary—or at least have the potential to be!

First, they tested sixteen hundred three- to five-year-olds and amazingly, 98% of them tested to be creative geniuses.

Next, they gave that same comprehensive testing to that exact group of youth when they were now eight to ten years old. Sadly, at this point, only 32% of these kids now tested as creative geniuses.

They waited another five years and gave the same children the tests once again. Now, at nearly fifteen years old, only 10% of the youth still graded out to be creative geniuses. What happened during that time?

More than two-hundred-thousand adults have taken the very same tests. Guess how many children grow up to still be creative geniuses as adults? Two percent! That's astounding and incredibly sad.

What should this teach us? Bottom line, it reminds us that God creates us one way, but the world is successfully making us something else. A study like this should open our eyes to the influence we are allowing the world to have in our children's lives, as well as what is being stolen from them. We are having the creative genius coached out of us on a daily basis through so many accepted, societal norms. Your kids are having their own unique genius stolen from them day after day. How much better would the world be, how much more light would there be, if kids were raised and empowered to still live freely from the image of their Creator that they originally arrived with? And how can we help restore that creative design to its rightful place in our children?

Their creative genius is still there. It's not gone, it's just dormant. It shuts down because the world slowly leads them into its carefully constructed norms and lanes of success, instead of blessing and empowering each child to freely be who God created them to be. On top of that, now the world is actively trying to coach them into counterfeit forms of difference and agenda. We are trading authentic, God-filled differences for the counterfeit differences of the world.

But we can still tap into that genius that's inside them! We as parents have the ultimate privilege of setting our kids free and empowering them to live out every bit God created them with. Just imagine what the world would look like. Imagine the life your child might live if we learn how to redeem the creative genius within them and coach it back to purposeful life!

THE CALIFORNIA GOLD RUSH:

The California Gold Rush is a famous movement of wealth that changed a nation. The draw of gold waiting to be unearthed was too much for some to resist, leading many to venture west into unknown territory in hopes of finding the immense, buried value that they heard was a possibility. The draw of the gold brought incredible amounts of people in search of this hopeful find, which led many people to leave their old, known life in search of a more glorious find.

In the small window of four years, 1848-1852, so many people flocked west that California's population grew from fourteen thousand people to two-hundred twenty-three thousand people; a growth so exponential that it left its mark on history—and not just because of the gold itself, but because of how that gold impacted the culture of everyday life. The rush to such a move changed California, thus changing the western United States as we know it, leaving our nation turned upside-down because of how people shifted population and culture in search of this hidden value.

The "Mother Lode" region of California was the primary target of the gold rush, even though that area spanned only five counties and an area that was a mere four miles wide and one hundred twenty miles long. The California Gold Rush is said to have brought forth 125 million troy ounces of gold, which in today's market would be worth over $2,600 per ounce.

But you know what is even more amazing? This historic, nation-altering discovery only extracted what is said to be approximately 10-20% of the gold that was waiting, available underground. That leaves 80% or more just waiting to be found. And if 10-20% made that kind of impact on a nation and caused that kind of a movement, what would've happened if they had found that other 80%?

That's a great picture of our generation of kids. Our children have a bright future full of possibilities. As is, they can change the communities and world all around them. But what if they're only living from 20% of what God actually created inside them? What if there's another 80% of that "creative genius" that is dormant, waiting to be found, extracted, and brought to the surface? What will happen when we learn to redeem that other 80% from within our kids, the same 80% that many of you as parents never had anyone to go after from within you.

If we redeem and empower that other 80%, it will be a far greater discovery than California's gold rush, the kind of world-altering value and light that can cast out darkness. It's just right there underneath the surface, waiting to be unearthed. Our kids are full of so much more than they know—so much more than we know! But that's what we can commit to redeeming together. Here's how.

THE CULTURE PURPLE:

My wife has been such an integral part of this journey of empowerment, of creative genius, finding the gold, and so much more. But despite being so in the middle of it, even she asked me one day, "If you've lost your creative genius, do you really think it's possible to get it back?" She knew the answer. But the question was genuine. The answer is an emphatic yes. And something we've used over the years to help look for or redeem that creative genius, that God-given purpose within the younger generation, is something we call "The Culture Purple."

In its most basic sense, the culture purple is a process of extraction. It is a principle of redeeming something that has more value than the eye can see. But it doesn't happen overnight. Purple has long been associated with royalty. However, it wasn't merely chosen for this role because of its specific color but because of the specific and valuable process that was necessary to produce this color otherwise it might have gone unseen by the world. Here is the breakdown according to Wikipedia:

"As early as the 15th century BC, the citizens of Sidon and Tyre, two cities on the coast of Ancient Phoenicia, (present-day Lebanon), were producing purple dye from a sea snail called the spiny dye-murex. The deep, rich purpled dye made from this snail became known as Tyrian purple.

The process of making the dye was long, difficult and expensive. Thousands of the tiny snails had to be found, their shells cracked, the snail removed. Mountains of empty shells have been found at the ancient sites of Sidon and Tyre. The snails were left to soak, then a tiny gland was removed, and the juice extracted and put in a basin, which was placed in the sunlight. There, a remarkable transformation took place.

In the sunlight, the juice turned white, then yellow-green, then green, then violet, then a red which turned darker and darker. The process had to be stopped at exactly the right time to obtain the desired color, which could range from a bright crimson to a dark purple, the color of dried blood. Then, either wool, linen or silk would be dyed. The exact hue varied between crimson and violet, but it was always rich, bright and lasting. Tyrian purple became the color of kings, nobles, priests and magistrates all around the Mediterranean."

For us today, purple is little more than a familiar color that only a handful of people still ascribe to the concept of royalty. But originally, it was anything but familiar because of the intricate method of extraction and processing what was inside those sea snails. Honestly, it's the same with our kids today. Few walk in their true "chosen" identity or calling because the unique genius inside them goes a lifetime unseen, or as the study shows us, intentionally buried. It waits for someone to see the royal potential who is willing to walk through that process for them, and with them. Our kids have something in them that is worth the greatest value possible, yet we live in a world that buries inside-out process under external labels and lesser pursuits. There is no quick fix to bring about what's inside our kids. Like purple, it's an enduring process. But if we will build a culture of extracting God-created value and surround our children and this whole next generation with such, we'll see God's promises come back to life in them and then through them.

At the beginning of this book, we dove into 1 Peter 2:9: *"...You are a chosen generation, a royal priesthood, a holy nation, His own special people, that you may proclaim the praises of Him who called you out of darkness into His marvelous light."*

There is a Hebrew phrase that translates to the beginning of that verse, "Am Segulah." It means to be "a chosen people," or, yes, it also means a "purple people." So, when we call forward a generation of our children to live out that chosen nature, we are actually praying for them to be a "purple people." We are hoping for them to emerge from that royal process that extracts what is on the inside to create that purple on the outside. These are the children of God that creation is crying out for in Romans 8. Many people were needed to walk through the process and produce purple for the royals at that time. And it is you and I as parents who are needed in order to walk through a similar method of extraction with our kids to pull out the treasures on the inside and see them become that chosen, royal, purple generation that has such a call in the times ahead.

That "process" will likely look different for each of you and your kids. It calls for us to adjust to our kids rather than just put them through a rote program. We can't rely on rigid, one-size-fits-all programs and yet still expect those programs to spit out original and creative people. Society does that too often, using cookie-cutter forms that do not exactly highlight unique, creative identity. Still, we want to give you an example of a place to begin with a few steps we have used before, though often applied in different ways. Each of these steps in the process is meant to be in the form of a question that gives your child, or you, permission to dream into that area of your own heart and life. We created a game built on this process that has been used all over the world, not to give youth or their parents the answers but to stimulate freedom and permission to dream and to unlock and find out what has already been within them the whole time. So, let's get started...

DREAM:

What do you want to give the world? If you could give the world and people anything, in a very big-picture sense, what would it be? Do you want to give love, hope, resources, leadership, second chances, big dreams, peace, joy, or....? Again, this one starts out very general for now, but let's start by finding out the essence of what change, opportunity or culture we want to see change the world and people around us. This question is less about a defined answer and more about charting the course of extracting what could be God-created dreams that are inside us.

COMPASSION:

Who does your heart naturally hurt for or feel drawn to help? Compassion is like tapping into a bigger engine that strengthens our love and multiplies our impact. It is a motive of greater love, not just out of doing something good, but out of an empathetic care for what other people are going through. Often, it is an area that you yourself went through and overcame, or that someone close to you went through. Thus, it gives you a heart for others who might be going through something similar. It can be a form of utilizing the power of your testimony. Maybe your compassion is for the homeless, for at-risk youth, for broken families, those impacted by illness or disease, those who have been through abuse, or any number of things. I find that we will often have tears or even anger rise in us in certain movies, each time driven by a specific hurt or injustice that grabs our heart. Pay attention to that. It is a clue as to who or what your compassion might be drawn towards. And if you can find and use your compassion, your impact and light will be that much greater because your love and motivation will be that much stronger. So many of Jesus' greatest miracles follow the passage saying, "He was moved with compassion."

PASSION:

This one is simple, but it's important. What do you love to do? What are you passionate about? Is it art, music, sports, business, building and construction, technology, media or something else? These things you love or are gifted in aren't just for you, but you can use them to reach others. We can help our kids to use their passions as ways to reach out to people and build a bridge to connect through that similar interest.

PURPOSE:

How will you make an impact? What method will you use, or what gifts and skillsets could you put to use? Could you start a business? Maybe open a facility for something. Perhaps you will write, speak, coach, mentor, or send resources and supplies. The important thing here is finding a vehicle that is natural to you and can be used to reach others.

NATIONS:

Simply, where do you have a heart for? Is it right there in your community? Is it somewhere else in your nation? Is it an African nation? What about an Asian nation or somewhere in South America or the Middle East? Is there somewhere your heart has always felt drawn towards? Why? One of the things my wife and I found in common when we first met was that we both felt a call to Africa. Since then, Africa has become a big part of our family and we've seen a lot of fruit and multiplication from there.

FIRST STEPS:

This one is simple and practical. But we always want to dream with actual action steps in mind. We want to make dreams possible. We want to make what is inside of you possible. So, we want to start by finding just one "First Step" you can take towards your dream or purpose? Maybe you could start by finding a mentor? Or perhaps by studying more about your area of compassion? Do you need training in an area of your Purpose or Passion? At first, it might be as simple as writing out a goal and a rough plan. The bottom line here is, find somewhere to start and take a first step so you or your kids don't just naturally return to old patterns.

PUTTING IT TOGETHER:

Then, as you start to process each of these areas or categories that you or your kids have inside them, you can allow them to simply be an exercise of dreaming, brainstorming and permission for what is on the inside to have space to emerge. Or you can put them all together. For instance, "I want to give (DREAM) to (COMPASSION) through (PASSION) by (PURPOSE) in (NATIONS) and my FIRST STEPS are (....) ?"

That might look like this: "I want to give HOPE to ORPHANS through ART by OPENING A FACILITY in an ASIAN NATION and my first steps are to WRITE OUT A GOAL AND A PLAN."

Whether you put it together or try and live out the exact path you build isn't really the point here. The goal is for you to use this to give your kids permission to dream into areas of life that are already inside them. Then, together, you can learn how they could creatively put those areas together to form a path that lets what God put inside them shine in the world! You or your child might choose one thing when going through this process, but then you go to bed at night and realize that now, more than anything, you're starting to think through those new, free questions on your own such as, "What do I want to give to the world?" Or "Who do I truly want to help?" The process is not about giving the answers but about giving your child freedom to start digging through that "other 80%" of the treasure that is still buried inside them and stoking the fires of their unique creative genius. Once they have that freedom, you continue to direct them to the Lord as their Source, help dream with God too about His purpose for their life, and all together, you begin to walk out what your child's light has the potential to be one step at a time, from the inside-out.

THE ARMY THAT SCATTERS DARKNESS:

Now, let's see how this comes alive and why the unique, creative purpose that is inside each of our children is so important and powerful. This strategy by the Lord found in Zechariah 1 blows me away.

"Then, I raised my eyes and looked, and there were four horns. And I said to the angel who talked with me, 'What are these?' So he answered me, 'These are the horns that have scattered Judah, Israel, and Jerusalem.' Then the Lord showed me four craftsmen.

And I said, 'What are these coming to do?'

So he said, 'These are the horns that scattered Judah, so that no one could lift up his head; but the craftsmen are coming to terrify them, to cast out the horns of the nations that lifted up their horn against the land of Judah to scatter it.'" (Zechariah 1:18-21)

Essentially, we have the four horns, or enemies, coming from the four corners of the earth—from every side—to try and scatter God's people. So, what does God do? He calls for the craftsmen, the "creatives," assuring Zechariah that those creative ones will be used to terrify the enemy and cast them out from their attack on God's people.

Going back to the creative genius study, and that which is created within your kids (and you, for that matter!), creatives don't just have to be artists and those who paint, sculpt, draw or the like. A craftsman or a creative is someone who can build something unique or operate in a variety of creative ways. They might innovate or invent something. That could be creativity in business strategy, creativity in economics, in teaching, parenting, and so much more. Creativity is boundless! Creativity and craftsmanship aren't necessarily what you do, but are how you do something, or how you process and think. The reality is that we are all made in the image of our Creator. We come from His likeness. Your kids come from His likeness. We are made with creative genius inside us, unique purpose that flows from our identity and when given the permission, freedom and the help it needs, is so strong that God can use it to literally terrify the enemy and push back the darkness coming against God's people. When we empower the creative genius and unique purpose from within our kids, we extract and build a light that terrifies darkness—just by helping them be who God created them to be in the first place.

No wonder the world is working so hard to steal our creative genius!

And I don't know about you, but that's about the coolest army I can imagine. I want to see it come to life. Our world needs it. Our world needs what God put within our kids. And we have the unique opportunity to redeem that genius, that purpose, out of the places it's been buried and see our kids shine so brightly that their light literally terrifies the enemy.

We are the parents of a generation of unending treasures that still haven't been found yet. The world is coaching it out of them, burying their light further, and giving them counterfeits instead. We as their parents, are going to be known as those who redeem what the world wants lost. We are going to be known as those who prepare the way for our kids and their generation through a purple, royal process and help them be free to fulfill every bit of creative potential they were born with.

WHERE TO START:

- Pray and ask God to show you the unique, creative genius within your kids. Begin to pray for them and their ability to live out the unique "genius" and purpose God created them with.

- Redeem: What is one specific area of creative genius in your child(ren) that God could use to shine in the world? How can you help highlight that for them, and how might you foster its freedom and growth?

- Sit down with your kids and begin to talk through the questions of the six-step process from the chapter. Dream. Compassion. Passion. Purpose. Nations. First Steps.

CHAPTER 5:

RE-ESTABLISH – An Identity Generation

I don't know if there has ever been such an obvious, unveiled war on identity as we are witnessing in the world today. Our kids are thrust into atmospheres and influences in every walk of life that are contending for confusion instead of security. If the world is contending for confusion, our kids, whether they can articulate it or not, are waiting for who will bring them the unseen, internal, secure foundation they need to live from. And other than God Himself, no one can bring that more authentically than parents because identity, or belonging, is rooted in the concept of family and one's place as a secure son or daughter of God.

When we struggle to give our kids that identity foundation to live from, they will wade further into the battle, looking for something to find identity in. They start to live for any identity they can latch onto, rather than living from the identity God created them in. As parents, if we do not proactively tackle this area in our kids' lives, something else will fill that place instead. And then, it is much more difficult to evict a counterfeit identity that someone has agreed with than it is to fill that spot with a true foundation in the first place.

Now, this is all easier said than done. Especially with the barrage of counterfeit bait being dangled in front of our kids from every source imaginable. Building identity is something that happens from the inside-out. That means it starts in the unseen, intangible places. Yet, as unseen as those places seem, there are very few thoughts that go through any of our heads each day that don't pass through our identity filter first. I mean, we rarely show that, let alone share that with anyone, all those little insecurities we keep in the dark that we're afraid people will see. So, we keep that area swept under the rug, even though we feel it at every turn. What is so difficult about that is that we live in a culture where almost everything is focused on externals and how those externals such as status, social media, jobs, money, looks, etc., seem to define us.

This is what brings us back to that word "Re-establish." In a world that tries to shake our core identity by showing us so many lesser, external or even counterfeit forms, we have to be even more intentional in everything we do with our kids to feed their true, created identity in Christ, and therefore re-establish a security in

their hearts that leaves them whole and satisfied, rather than hungry for all the bait that is being dangled in front of their face each day.

GOLD VS. CASH:

One of my favorite ways to define or explain how to differentiate between true identity and worldly identity is to look at the differences between gold and cash. Why? Truly, it's as simple as the fact that one is a natural resource with intrinsic value, while the other is man-made and has zero natural value.

If you continue to look at it, you realize that gold is something that is often hidden beneath the surface. It is hard to find for many. It is often covered up by dark or rocky substance, and you have to know what you're looking for in order to find it. It has value because of its nature that goes beyond what man ascribes to it in the moment. And it is lasting. You can put gold in a fire only for it to be purified by it, and despite the fire it retains value. Gold goes unfound and unused by most of the population.

Cash currency, on the other hand is something that is literally printed on demand. It is paper in substance, is flaunted everywhere, by everyone, in different forms. It can be burned up and never heard from again, yet all the while most of the population spends day and night trying to get more of it, often feeling like we'll get worth from or be defined by it.

Clearly, gold represents our true, authentic, created identity. It is something that we all are born with, that often sits hidden, unfounded within the innermost parts of us. It is who God created us to be in His image. It can't be taken away from us, but we can unfortunately ignore its value and place in our lives. While cash represents the lesser and even counterfeit identities we seek to gain in the eyes of the world and others all the time, we still try to get more of it in order to prove some external identity to onlookers who haven't been taught to recognize that they, and you, are already sitting on a pile of gold that's worth much more than anything we could ever gain in the world.

What if you saw someone who you knew was sitting on a mountain of gold, yet despite that gold you watched them spend their whole life striving to chase after more and more cash to try and fulfill what they fear they are lacking? You would either feel bad for that person, or honestly might think they are either ignorant, or quite frankly, an idiot. How could you live like you are in poverty while sitting on a pile of gold? Sadly, isn't that what the world teaches us and our kids to do? The world tantalizes us with externals, teaches us to measure by what we have and/or do on the outside, all the while making us forget or ignore the pile of genuine wealth that we each are born with on the inside.

From an identity perspective, far too often, we are still chasing cash while sitting on a pile of gold. It's not that hard for any of us to do, either. If our identity is not filled up as parents, we will often try and live for something that we already have. We will aim for success while kind of forgetting the greater success that's found at home in our families. We will aim for money at the expense of valuing our spouse and children. And if we as parents still struggle with this, what example—or identity—are we passing down to our kids? And what are we going to do about it? How are we going to help our kids live from the gold they already have, instead of living for the cash that will leave them chasing the wind for a lifetime? They will follow our lead. Our example of living out of our own identity in Christ is the best tool we possess to help our children live the same. Because the truth is, it's hard to be a father or mother if we haven't first become a true son or daughter. When we know who we are in God's family, we start to naturally reproduce that in our family as well.

WHO VS. DO:

One of the most common tug-o-wars over our identity, especially for us parents, is the place we allow to be the source of our identity, knowingly or unknowingly. As we've talked about from a variety of angles, the world we live in is built to make us gravitate towards finding our identity in what we do, and being successful at such. Likewise, as believers in Jesus, we know the truths that say that is only by grace that we are saved, yet even in that situation, the longer we follow the Lord we often end up lapping back around to try to earn God's love and pleasure through our works or by somehow proving that we are acceptable. That's how easy a trap it is to fall back into.

For example, I am an author of more than fifteen books and a father of eight children (even though several aren't children anymore). Society normally wants us to find worth and identity out of what we do, and therefore it could be easy to get such worth and identity based on the apparent outward success of my books. And then, I could easily get more secure or insecure by my success or provision as said author. (Though I can assure you from that experience that being an author is definitely NOT an area where you want to find your worth and identity, lol). However, being a "dad" of eight kids, and now a grandpa to two grandkids is genuinely a part of who I am. The world typically appreciates us more for writing a bunch of books than it does for having a bunch of amazing, invaluable kids. And sadly, we often take on that same value system without even realizing it far too often, even though it's not what we would really believe.

What we do is important. The Bible reminds us that faith without works is dead. But there is an important order to said being and doing. Who we are comes first, then, what we do naturally flows out of who we are and usually—hopefully—is made better because of it! Being an author doesn't really make me a better dad but being a secure dad who values my kids more than my work or the world's perception of me certainly makes me a better author. When I work or write to gain success or money, it doesn't go very far in the ways that count. But when I write out of my father's heart and identity, it infuses said writing with something that goes beyond any skill, or lack thereof, and multiplies much further in the ways that mean the most. Who we are, our identity, has more to give than our hands do. And, truly, we reproduce who we are much more naturally than we reproduce what we do.

This is such a vital area for us to reproduce in and for our kids. But first, it must be genuinely alive in us. As we've discussed, our kids are in the middle of both the hope and the battle for their future, and their identity is usually the playing field that is being attacked most often, and most underhandedly. The enemy wants little more than to shake the security of your kids' mindset in this way because then they will be far more prone to all his other wiles in the world. But if your kids know who they are and even more importantly whose they are, the darkness of the world won't be able to shake them; rather, they will be part of the generation who are children of light, pushing back darkness simply because WHO God created them to be has been set free to lead the way from the inside-out.

Even Jesus, the Son of God, had this area filled up by the Father as He set out in this world. At His baptism, before Jesus started His ministry before He did any of His works or miracles, the Father found this area of establishing WHO His Son is to be so important that He practically stopped time and opened the clouds to speak over Him, *"This is My Beloved Son, in Whom I Am well pleased."* The Father was pleased with Who Jesus was before He accomplished any of His mission. The Father wanted the Son to be so filled up with the identity of Who He is, that He could live from that place throughout His entire life and mission on earth. Jesus never did one thing while having to prove to Himself or His Father Who He was because the Father already made sure He was secure in that area. And everything else would flow from that place. A good Father brings identity to their family.

If Jesus had that area filled up fully as the Son of God even, how much more do we, and especially our kids, need that foundation given the utmost attention as they venture out into the world each day. If we will be proactive like the Father was there with Jesus to set our kids up with a fulfilled identity, then our kids will be set up to be proactive in not conforming to the battles of the world each day but overcoming it, instead.

OUR MOST COMMON & MISUSED TOOL:

One of the simplest, yet often hardest places to begin is with what is one of our most familiar, readily used tools in our toolbox. Yet this tool is something we all unintentionally misuse all the time: Our words.

Words are one of the most powerful yet frivolous things we have, and as simple as they seem they can be one of the most important when building or re-establishing identity. The Bible itself says that life and death are in the power of the tongue. The great thing is that we have control over our words, the hard part is that we don't always take control over our words. In the world we live in, with pressures, expectations and busyness to the max, it becomes far too easy for our words to be led by our reactions, instead of that which we are pro-actively building and truly believe in. And often, those closest to us such as our spouse and our kids are the ones who take the brunt of those reactionary words.

The reality is that words are a sword that we are learning to wield. We say things that we don't mean in the heat of the moment, but even when we don't mean to, those words usually still mean something to whoever is on the receiving end. It doesn't even have to be a big, angry or negative lashing out, it's often just those quick, impatient moments when we don't give ourselves time to think what our words might accomplish once they're released from our mouth. Words build identity. They create positives, or negatives, and they also affirm positives and negatives that are already there. So, when one of those moments happens that our child makes a mess or causes an inconvenience with a small accident, we might be tempted to say, "Agh, you always do that!" And while we're just processing through our own frustration, we forget in the moment that, as parents, our children are being shaped by all those little things we say. To us, it's a flippant phrase that we didn't really mean. To our child, it's a label that sticks and becomes a filter for many of their thoughts and actions. The above reaction tells our kids what we think of them, "that they always do that." This actually just sets them up to either:

A. Do that thing even more often, or...

B. Start to operate out of fear that they will do that, which creates a wall in our future freedom of communication and operation with them.

Or what if they keep pestering you and asking about the same thing, or many different things, while you are busy on something that needs focus. Eventually, we might get to a point of a semi-controlled version of a snap. We are careful to avoid telling them to shut up, but instead we say, "I don't have time for that right now," or "I need you to just leave me alone so I can think." Look at those statements and think about how our kids might process them beyond those moments. Is it possible they start thinking, "I should just be quiet all the time," "I'm a bother to Mom/Dad," or some other label they take on about their communication or their connection with you. The last thing we want our kids to create an internal agreement with is the idea that we don't have time for them. We certainly don't feel that way, but sometimes it's what we tell them in unintentional ways. As hard as it can be in the moment, all it takes is for us to just take a few seconds of reset in our head, acknowledge them enough to validate their worth beyond the moment, and create a connect that can be followed up on later.

For us as parents, it can be difficult to stop before our reaction and think to ourselves, "what am I building here?" But it's a worthwhile moment if we will take it. When we utilize that patience, it is there that we find grace. Once we drink of a little of that grace for ourselves, then we have grace to offer our kids as well. We can, of course, still address the situation with our kids, but that patience and grace helps us to re-organize our thoughts and use them to build instead of accidentally tear down. It helps us to take the opportunity to coach our child forward with how they could handle that situation rather than use our words to compound how they feel after whatever happened. In those moments, we can use our own internal filter of, "what identity am I building by saying this?"

The hope for all of us is to always seek to use our words to be constructive and build our children up. Our kids have so much value that calls for us to be patient in those little, tense moments. Again, it's not always angry words, more often than not it's just small familiar phrases that are cultural or were passed down from our own parents and what they didn't realize they were speaking over us. How often in life did someone—whether a friend, a parent, a boss, or some random stranger even—say one little thing to you that somehow stuck in your head and became a filter for what you feel insecure about or an area you started to try and prove yourself in? I think we've all had small words become big places of identity. They become cracks in our foundation when they could have built something on top of that foundation. Little words and negative tones have shaped all of us to an extent. So, as parents, they become a small but mighty tool that's important to learn how to wield.

On the flip side, it is in those seemingly insignificant moments with our kids where we can utter small, significant words that they can build off of. When you catch your child being thoughtful, it's making sure we don't just gloss over it but take the moment to let them know you saw that in them, and remind them, "you're such a thoughtful person, I love that about you!" Or when they want to help clean up or do something with you that might actually make your task more difficult, it's highlighting that desire with something like, "I am so thankful for how you're always willing to help and serve others." It can be the smallest things, but when we pause to acknowledge and then speak to those things, we let them know those are important building blocks that emerge from who they are, and who you hope they continue to be.

We're not talking all rosy or participation trophy-type words either. We don't want to give a false sense of identity in the other way. We're talking about what direction our words lead our children, both in times of encouragement, correction, or just answers to their many questions. Because if we want them to walk the best path God created them for amidst the battle all around them, our words as parents and what those words are filled with just might pro-actively be the answer they need to get through one of those battles they face down the road. The goal is to use our words to not only affirm who our kids already are, but to call them higher and forward for the future. In fact, our words in one small moment are truly what build their future. Those words help determine where they have strength in that battle of identity. But first, that battle starts with us as parents in our own hearts and heads. Establishing and re-establishing our children's identity is a moment-by-moment opportunity throughout our day, and we're never off the clock.

At the same time, it's not just the words we speak, either. We try and stay keenly aware to the words our kids are using. If my ten-year-old says something in reaction to something he did, such as "I always mess up at this," or makes some other blanket statement about himself or someone else, we try to gently highlight what he just said and remind him to think about what he is speaking over himself or someone else. It's too easy to make a "who I am or am not" label for us or someone else based on something we did or didn't do well. It's one more way, unfortunately, where we allow what we do to overtake who we are. Just because we struggled once doesn't mean we can't grow. It's important that our kids start to understand the power of their words over themselves. Plus, when we remind them how and/or why to rephrase their words, at the same time, we're reminding them the value of who they by taking the time to focus on it together. Taking that time with them isn't nitpicking if we handle it constructively, rather, it's helping understand their value and use words that live up to their value.

Whether we are disciplining our child, correcting them, coaching them, encouraging them or blessing them, our words should point them back to the plumbline of who we believe God created them to be. A plumbline is a vertical alignment and earth's center of gravity. And that's our call as parents, to call our kids back to vertical alignment with their heavenly Father, centered in Him and who He sees them to be. Everything in the world is competing to speak to our kids' identity, but it is us, as parents who have the right of first refusal and the ability to shape not only our kids' future but the world's future through their lives.

Identity can be one of the biggest battles we face in the world, and hopefully, we can win that battle before it even begins for our children by re-investing in them every day with something simple as simple and save-able as our words.

WHERE TO START:

- Spend time praying for the gold in your child(ren) and how to bring it out. Pray for your kids to see themselves the way God sees them.

- Re-Establish: How do you need to re-establish your own identity in Christ to reproduce true identity in your kids? How can you model that?

- Try and find one time each day when you re-phrase your normal reaction to your kids into words that intentionally build their identity and future instead.

CHAPTER 6:

RE-INVEST – The Art of Empowerment

As you know, the value within each of our kids is immeasurable, and we, as parents, have been given the privilege of stewarding that value. I know the famous parable of the talents is usually reserved for financial discussions, but its angle on stewardship is even more important when discussing our children, as it is considered the highest level of stewardship Biblically. And since our kids have the highest value possible, beyond what we even know sometimes, the parable is a perfect path forward if we are going to empower our kids to fully live out who God created them to be.

Summarizing this parable from Matthew 25:14-30, as you likely know, we have three people who each have been entrusted with varying amounts of talents. One was given five, another was given two, and the other was given one. The one who had five talents used that value to go and acquire five more, and the master was very pleased. The servant who was given two talents went and multiplied that into two additional talents, four in total. Again, the master was pleased. But the servant who was only given one talent feared losing what he was given, so he buried that talent to protect it so as not to suffer loss. The master was so upset with him that he called him a "wicked and lazy servant," and then proceeded to take even that one talent away and give it to the servant who had ten.

I probably don't even need to try and explain how this relates to stewarding and empowering our children. No doubt you can see clearly that stewarding with fear instead of faith was what displeased the master most, the fact that he had sat on the value he was entrusted with. And if our children are truly our greatest heritage and value, I wonder if we shouldn't be thinking along these lines as we raise them. Are we simply protecting them or teaching them how to just "fit in" with the world and its paths of success? Or are we empowering our children from an early age to recognize the kind of value God put inside them, helping them learn early on how to use that value purposefully? Essentially, we are called to re-invest in, not just protect, the value that God already invested into our kids. This goes back to that question we posed earlier in the book; Are we playing offense or defense? Better yet, are we teaching our kids to play offense or defense?

Often, our reasoning for not empowering our kids jumps right to the "well, they're not ready yet," line of thinking. But, why not? Why aren't they ready? We're not asking them to go off into some new battle, they're already in that battle every day whether we like it or not. And when you look at how Jesus operated with the disciples, He did far more than just teach and equip them—He gave them opportunity, even before they might be ready. That's empowerment. And He did so not later in life when they were mature and grown up, He empowered them while He was still walking alongside them, helping them find their way and picking them up if—or when—they fail (cough, Peter). From the moment Jesus called the disciples, He didn't just say, "Well, after 20 years in my program, you should be ready to step out on your own." Not at all, in fact, from moment one He was already giving them vision for their calling by referring to them as "fishers of men," before they had any idea what that was let alone being ready to walk in such.

In fact, it was early on in Jesus' time with them that He ramped things up a bit quickly on the empowerment front. At the very end of Matthew 9 Jesus said to His disciples, *"The harvest truly is plentiful, but the laborers are few. Therefore, pray the Lord of the harvest to send out laborers into His harvest."*

And then, in verse 1 of Matthew 10, Jesus called His twelve disciples to Him and started giving them power, much of the same power that He was walking in. Notice He called them disciples as He gathered them. Then He gave them power. Immediately after, in verse 2, He suddenly started to call them apostles. So, one moment He says that the harvest is huge, and we need to pray for more workers out there. The next moment He's answering His own prayer by giving power to His disciples, which suddenly upgraded their calling into apostles. Jesus didn't just disciple those entrusted into His care, He empowered them! He gave them opportunity early on in their walk with Him. Many of us are praying for change in our homes, our schools, community, churches and the like, but what if our kids are the ones who hold much of what can be the answer to those prayers? What if we're sitting on some of the Lord's greatest value that's waiting to be empowered to shine? Whether through the parables He told, or through the actions He modeled, Jesus made it clear that He wasn't just looking to coddle or protect a bunch of disciples, He was empowering those He saw value in to live from that value and learn how to multiply it in the world.

Now, empowerment can be hard. That's a huge reason why many people don't engage with it. Well, that and the fact that the word has been somewhat tarnished by certain movements in the world that are trying to empower people in the wrong spirit. But that's even more reason we need to take empowerment back to where it was intended. There's no exact science for empowerment. Notice how Jesus went about it with the disciples, there wasn't some rote, cookie cutter program or format. Nope, it was just a raw struggle-bus of life on life building people on the right foundation, re-shaping their perspective and empowering them to live and multiply from that foundation. He saw value in people, and step-by-step re-invested in that value. That's what our kids are waiting for, too! They crave that kind of purpose.

So, if empowerment isn't a science, then it must be an art form. There are all kind of ways to engage our kids in small and big ways to start to empower them. It might start through our words or by including them in more forward discussions or family purpose. It might be giving them opportunity for more purposeful responsibility, a journal to start processing or praying about God's purpose for their lives or giving them permission to dream into God's possibilities through their life, or even dream together with you. One of the greatest, dreaming, white-board times I've ever had in my life wasn't with a room full of adults or other leaders—but with eight orphans in rural Ethiopia who ranged from ages 8-13 years old.

We had been working with them for a couple of months, teaching them to hear God's voice and dream with God about His purpose for their lives. At the same time, most days of the week, we were out walking the streets of Addis Ababa to reach out to new kids who literally lived on those streets. One weekend, we were privileged to have all eight of the kids from the orphanage over to our home for what we called a "Pray & Play" weekend. It was a wild, messy, life-filled weekend that ended up being one of the best weekends of our lives! But at one point during the weekend, we talked with those eight "orphans," (I put it in quotes because even though the world would call them orphans, those eight kids were anything but orphans in God's eyes and were already walking as children of God.) discussing with them the kids on the streets. We asked the eight kids, "If you know how God sees you, and how much He loves you, how do you think He feels about all those kids on the streets who are your same age and growing up in very similar, hard circumstances?"

From there, we gave each of the kids a pen and a piece of paper. We asked them to take the next hour, spread out around our home and property, pray, and ask God this question:

"How do You, God, see the kids on the streets, and what do You want to say to them?"

Then, whatever they felt was God's response of what He would want to say to the kids on the streets, we asked them to write a letter to those kids from the Father's perspective and what He wanted to speak over their lives.

After the hour was up, we brought all the kids back together in front of a big whiteboard. It was there that we started to ask the kids to share with us what they felt the Father wanted to say to the kids on the streets, and we jotted down their notes on the whiteboard. What came out of their hearts and mouths was astounding! We were so blown away that we eventually compiled their letters and notes into a bigger letter that we had translated and printed to take to the kids on the streets. Before we knew it, copies of that letter were being shared all over the streets of the capital of Ethiopia. It wasn't our words; it was the kids from the orphanage. They were reaching the Father's heart all the way past their young age, past their circumstances, and shining light into the streets, culture, and into many of the same dark circumstances that they, too, had been growing up with. It was in them the entire time, they just had to be given the opportunity.

For me personally, being empowered at a young age by my parents, by teachers, youth leaders and others were some of the most formative pathways of my life. I learned so much from trial, and error, and being given opportunity to dream beyond my current ceiling was part of how I learned to hear God's voice in a way that called me up higher and higher with Him.

A BLANK CANVAS:

With the art form that empowerment becomes, I've often used a blank canvas as an analogy, if not an actual tool to help try and bring it to life. In theory alone, you can ask someone to imagine what they would do if they had a blank canvas in front of them, with total liberty to ask for or dream into whatever they like. The funny thing is that most people openly dream of having such a free, blank check in front of them, yet the reality is that many of us don't know what to do with such a blank canvas when it's finally put in front of us. That in itself makes the blank canvas exercise important. The goal isn't necessarily to get your exact answer, rather, the hope is to start to give yourself permission to dream and to look more intently at what God has already put inside you. Once given that permission, it forces you to not be so frivolous with your thoughts or dreams but helps you prioritize how you really want to spend your blank canvas.

This is a great exercise to give your kids, too. It is an exercise of giving them vision and a place where they can start to imagine how they might use the value that is within them, even if just in concept. Truly, it's a practical way to dream and to do so while playing together at the same time. You can use it with specifically directed questions as well, such as what we asked the kids from the orphanage about the kids on the streets. You can open up big picture questions in the world, or their lives, that need answers. Then, use the canvas, real or imaginary, to bring possible purposes and solutions to life—while using your creativity of course! Your child is, after all, a creative genius.

One way we have done this was by giving actual blank canvases to a fairly big group. Then, we asked them to paint or draw on the canvas whatever hope looks like for them. This wasn't easy at first. Many didn't know where to start, and others didn't feel like they were comfortable even trying to draw or paint. Often, we're so not accustomed to being given freedom that, at first, we don't even know how to use it or where to start. But as we got going, it was so beautiful to watch what each person put on their canvas and then to listen to them describe it afterwards and explain their "why." Some of those who had the hardest time getting started now did not want to stop, or even wanted to do it again more often. And the uniqueness of each creation, not to mention the hope motive behind them, were so encouraging. There was a diverse beauty in what a vision of hope would look like, whether for themselves and their calling or for the world in general.

What's so important about that for us to remember as parents is that often when we start to empower our kids towards purpose or future, we do so by encouraging them to paint what we see as hope for their lives. And while our intentions are always good in that way, to truly empower our kids to be who God created them to be we need to make sure we don't paint that picture for them, that we don't hand them a paint-by-number canvas or have them follow us along like a painting class. Instead, we should give them the freedom to dream with God into their own blank canvas, as this helps them start to find their own vision with God for their lives. In my best intentions, I can still be a limit or a ceiling on who God created my child to be. I have to give them permission to walk through that process personally, encouraging them but directing them to find God's picture of hope for their life instead of our picture of hope for their life. That's where empowerment truly comes alive. *It's where we can empower our kids not from our own strength but from God's strength.* And that is the point where their special, unique light that God put inside them fully, and freely, has the chance to come alive and start to shine in the world!

Empowerment as an art form doesn't just stop with how we have to adjust to each individual and their unique makeup. It also adjusts based on seasons. Empowerment isn't just a task we "do" consistently with our kids. It is a mindset of forward growth and purpose, which usually occurs in ebbs and flows. There is a time to exercise your growth forward, and there are other seasons where the act of pruning is just as much part of empowering someone forward. There are times when we've really been able to bring our kids into the middle of world harvest fields at a young age, and there have been other seasons where they are learning and living planted right where they are at. The two work in conjunction with each other. The key is that both are done with forward empowerment in mind. The more still or "normal" seasons are an active kind of waiting, not stagnant, but moving forward in more internal and intangible kinds of ways. It goes back to the verse we talked about previously from Hebrews 6:12 regarding the need for both faith and patience to inherit the promises. Both have their place, as long as both are going in the same direction towards the promise.

HARNESSING FAILURE:

One of the reasons people often gravitate away from empowering others is they are afraid that if the person they empower fails, that it will be tied to their reputation as a parent or a leader. This is one more thing that stems from the externally based, results-oriented culture we live in. Such measurements rob our ability to use the freedom we've been given. They keep us in fear, and once again, they keep us on defense. When we don't empower someone because of those types of fears, we've already empowered failure before we ever even gave them a chance to fail. At that point, it is us that has failed them because we were afraid they would fail us. But the truth is, failure is a natural and healthy part of the process.

Life and purpose are in no way a straight line. And I would rather someone have the chance to fail early on, fail for the right reasons and with the right people around them. Mix all that together and you have a recipe for growth. But when we hold people back from the freedom required to fail, we're only postponing their failure until a later date when they may run through a barrier on their own, maybe for the wrong reasons, and potentially with the wrong people around them. That mixture can be way harder and longer to recover from. But failure in a good setup is part of learning the right way forward. In fact, a lot of times when failure happens in that way, it's so small that it doesn't even have to look, feel or smell like failure, because it just starts to blend in as one more stepping-stone to leap from to the next one. Check out these "famous failures" below and see how their area of strength or success was built upon what may have started out as an area of weakness.

Albert Einstein: He couldn't speak until he was nearly four years old, and his teachers said he would never amount to much. Then, he became a world-famous theoretical physicist and Nobel Prize winner.

Michael Jordan: After being cut from his high school basketball team, he went home, locked himself in his room and cried. Later, he became a six-time NBA World Champion and five-time NBA Most Valuable Player.

Walt Disney: He was fired from a newspaper job for "lacking imagination" and having "no original ideas." Can you imagine someone saying that about Walt Disney now? He lived totally the opposite of those words and became the creator of Disney, Mickey Mouse and won many, many Academy Awards.

Thomas Edison: A teacher told him he was "too stupid to learn anything" and that he "should go into a field where he might succeed by virtue of his pleasant personality" instead. And then ,as we know, he went on to invent the light bulb.

There are many more famous success stories just like these. Thomas Edison once said, "I haven't failed. I've just found 10,000 ways that don't work." I love that! And honestly, that's exactly how I feel most of the time. Failure is not a dead end, and it's certainly not final, either. Failure is a gust of learning that propels us forward. And if that is true, then empowerment shouldn't be such a scary thing either. And that's why we as parents are best suited to empower our kids early on while we can give them the right set up to fail well and then shine even better! It also gives us as parents time to learn the most fruitful ways to empower them well.

Truly, there are so many ways we can and will empower our kids, that is, if and when we pick up the mindset that empowering our kids is a good thing. Because when you do, you'll come up with ways to empower your kids I couldn't even begin to list or share about here.

Once that light comes on in you, the light will start shining that much brighter through your kids as well.

That said, I want to finish this chapter by sharing the most empowering thing I ever learned while growing up and what I believe has been the most empowering thing I could give to my kids or others we've worked with as well.

LISTENING TO GOD:

One year, for Mother's Day I was stumped as to what to write in the card for my mom. Usually, words like that come easy to me, and there are few more worthy of such words than my mom. But that was just it, everything I could think to say sounded like trivial words of blessing or encouragement. I started praying about it and that's when it hit me, I remembered a consistent comment my mom said often, "I wish I could meet all your needs." I'm sure many parents have wished the same. But what struck me most was realizing that I could tell her that she had; my mom had met all my needs.

Now, I know that sounds crazy, and even unhealthy, as no one person can or should meet all someone else's needs. However, this was different. One of the most important things my mom had taught me, starting from an early age, was how to listen to God. Through practice, example, encouragement and more, she had taught me how to slow my typically high-end energy and drive, be still, and know God's voice. And if I know how to hear God's voice, I have everything I could ever need. Jesus Himself when being tempted by the enemy to satisfy his need for food responded, "Man does not live by bread alone but by every word that proceeds from the mouth of God." If I know how to hear His voice, then I know when to go forward in faith, I know when to wait, I know when to go left, I know when to go right. God is my Provider of everything I could need, and more. By learning to hear His voice, I knew how to stay in alignment with Him, how to join Him, and how to receive from Him in each season.

Hearing God's voice isn't some trivial thing, obviously. And some people even scoff at the idea. But God is always speaking, we're just not always taught how to listen or to take the time to listen. To know His voice, we have to know His word in the Bible, it's the only way to discern if it's God speaking, self's voice, or the enemy whispering lies. God does not change and His voice will always align with His word, His character, and His nature.

Hearing His voice also requires patience. We live in a world that is growing more and more dependent on instant gratification, and needing the next thing to get that dopamine hit in the brain that we start to feed off. Culture today is contrary to the patience required to hear His voice, so it takes discipline to wait through all the distractions around us, and the distractions within us. Waiting on God and His voice is something I've practiced now for most of my life, yet I still must push through those distractions the first five, ten, even fifteen minutes—swatting them away like flies that are trying to steal my stillness. And, based on that, listening to God requires practice. It is a practice of knowing Him and getting to know how He speaks to you uniquely. He knows you better than you know yourself, wants to reveal Himself to you, and knows just how to do it. We just need to spend enough time with Him to, like Jesus said, be one of His sheep that knows His voice.

We started practicing this with our firstborn daughter, Mercy, when she was just four years old. It wasn't about going after some grandiose encounter or word from the Lord, it was just about taking the time and starting to practice together. We kept it so simple at first. At four years old, she and I sat on the couch, and I said, "Ok, we're going to take 30 seconds to be quiet with God and listen. I just want you to ask Him one question; "God, do you love me?" We spent the 30 seconds in silence together and when we both opened our eyes, I asked her, "So, what did God say?" "Yes," she said sweetly, "He said He loves me." So, we took it a step further. Now I told her we would spend one minute being quiet in prayer to listen to God. This time I encouraged her, "Ask God what He wants to tell you today." So, she did. And when the minute was up her answer blew me away. "God said, I have a Spirit inside me that helps me to be good." Wow, I thought, we hadn't even talked about the Holy Spirit in those terms up to that point. But God was revealing Himself to her. As many people have said, "there is no junior Holy Spirit." We simply must lead our kids into such an opportunity. It is one of the best ways we can empower them because it takes them beyond us and lets them learn to go straight to the Source for themselves.

We've done some of the same exercises of waiting and listening to God with Junior High students, High School kids, with college students, adults and with orphans and street kids. In fact, it became one of the most life and community-changing practices we engaged in with those eight to thirteen-year-old kids in the orphanage in Ethiopia, and with the kids on the streets too. We watched God meet them with specific answers of provision, things they usually would beg for, all starting with learning God's voice in their own hearts. We gave the kids in the orphanage "God Journals" to write down what

He was speaking to them, and we were always amazed at what they would teach us, and one another, even at such a young age.

Empowering our kids and the next generation to listen to God is one of the greatest gifts we can give them and one of the most powerful ways for them to learn how and where to shine the light He has already put inside them. If you truly want to empower your children, simply turn off the noise, get on your face with them, and practice being still and listening to God together. We, as parents, need it as much as they do.

WHERE TO START:

- Pray over your kids about how to empower their purpose. Try this every day for one week. Ask God how to empower each, and then pray for them in those ways before you put empowerment into action.

- Re-Invest: Find a hidden value in your kids that they might not be using yet, such as their creative genius, and look at what you have in your hands that you could use to invest in that value.

- Take time to practice listening to God on your own, then, include your child(ren) and practice together. When you finish, ask questions and discuss.

CHAPTER 7:

RENDER – The Father's Blessing

"Render" isn't a word I hear used all that often. I imagine you don't either. In fact, the most common way I hear the word "render" used is in regard to when Jesus said, "render to Caesar what is Caesar's," while speaking about the need to pay taxes. Of course, this chapter has nothing to do with that, but I do like the directive here to render to someone what is due them. And I want to apply it to our kids. We should absolutely want to learn how to render to our children all that God meant for their lives. We can either stand in the way unintentionally and block what God means for our kids, or we can be active participants and render to our kids' heart and identity what the Father says over their lives and help facilitate the purpose He has for them. I'm sure most of you certainly wouldn't disagree with that on the surface but putting it to action is something that most of our kids are quietly waiting for.

When I was about to turn sixteen, before handing me a license or keys to a car, my dad wanted me to learn more about what many refer to as "The Father's Blessing," and its place in families and heritage since Abraham became a father of nations. Back then, that kind of blessing could be looked at by us today as a birthright formality, or just another religious exercise empty of practical meaning. But my mom and dad wanted to change that. My dad did ask me to go back and read some of the origins of the "Blessing" story among Isaac and his two sons, Esau and Jacob. But that was only so I would understand the background as my parents were preparing to build on it in a fresh way.

I read the story, and it was pretty familiar, didn't jump off the page in any new way. But my dad told me that for my sixteenth birthday party that they wanted to give me somewhat of a "Blessing" party, where I could invite one friend my age and then they would bring together a group of family friends to join for the evening. Now you must understand, for my thirteenth birthday I had a city-wide scavenger hunt with about eighty kids between school, youth group and the neighborhood. So, in my mind I was expecting my sixteenth to go up a notch in some way. That said I was a little hesitant. But I could see the importance in my dad's eyes, so, reluctantly, I agreed.

The night came around for my blessing and I didn't know exactly what to expect. I had been growing a lot that past year in my personal relationship with the Lord, but my parents were still wanting to see "the true Joey" they had always known me to be re-emerge a little more. See, as a kid, I was what they always called "a pied-piper leader." I wasn't trying to lead, but would naturally gather and galvanize friends, younger and older, in a variety of directions and would lead in similar ways at school and in sports. But something had dampened that those past few years, not in a rebellious way, but more of a cover my light to fit in and be cool kind of way. They missed who they truly knew me to be, and they had both prayed long and hard about this blessing to help call me forward again, hoping I would return to the free Joey they had always seen naturally shine God's light.

The night of my birthday blessing arrived, and I really didn't know what to expect. My dad and mom, however, had spent a lot of time preparing both in prayer, and my dad spent weeks, if not months, writing out the blessing he/they would speak over me that night. As the night got started family friends went around the room, each taking turns speaking different kinds of blessing, encouragement and affirmations over my life; things they had seen in me and/or things they were praying for my life. Then, when it reached my dad, he and my mom stood behind me and began to read the Father's Blessing he had prepared over me, in front of all these witnesses.

I can't state strongly enough that there was no one dramatic moment of change that night, but what I can tell you in an even stronger way is that something was unlocked and set free in me in an even more profound way over the coming months. The blessing spoke to who I was and what they saw in my life, as well as what they believed about my future. They blessed me for who I was, and more specifically, for the unique son they saw God created me to be. They went into specific attributes of my demeanor, my personality, areas they saw developing and affirmed their presence to help me fulfill who God made me to be. One specific part that has always stuck out was where my dad wrote:

"I hope you never believe that just because you're not like me in every area of life that I think you're a lesser person. That's a common belief among sons of "Type-A" dads. In fact, I believe the very best hope for the LeTourneau name lies in the very ways that you are different from me."

I didn't realize in the moment how powerful and revolutionary that statement was and still is to this day. Because of the insecurities and fears we all battle to an extent; it can be hard even to bless the similarities in someone else. Yet, here was my dad saying that our family name would actually be better because of the ways God made me different than him. It requires a lot of security in oneself to say that. In essence, my dad was giving me permission not to try and measure up to him, let alone to the expectations of society. Instead, he was blessing me to run my own unique race with the Lord and fully, freely be who God made me to be.

As much as it wasn't some sudden change that I was aware of, the blessing did something that night—and continued to do something— that reached down and flipped some kind of belief and freedom switch in me. That next year my parents watched "Joey" come back to life. They watched me shake off those typical teenage efforts to fit in or compare myself with others. They saw my already growing relationship with the Lord hit overdrive, and passions and purposes they always believed were in me started to find their way out to the surface again. They watched me surge forward beyond what they might have even hoped because now, I wasn't just being led by them, as wonderful as they are, I was personally being infused and led by the Lord Himself as my Source.

My parents rendered to me the type of blessing, much more than words or religious exercise, that God had always breathed towards my life and released me to God so I could live the Father's best, rather than their best. A couple of years later, my mom told me a story about my dad during that revived year after my blessing, a story that I was unaware had such an effect on him. As God further grabbed my heart that year after the blessing, one night I emerged from a prayer time around midnight so sure of God's call on my life in "ministry" of some sorts. I had to tell them! So, I ran upstairs, knocked slightly, but burst through their doors into the dark room where my parents were sleeping soundly. Without going into much detail at all, I told them of God's call for my life and my "Yes" to the Lord. And just as quickly, I left their room so they could go back to sleep and I could simmer down in prayer with the Lord myself.

There's much more to the story still that I'll share about soon, but when my mom told me more about my dad's reaction to that night after I burst through their doors, it helped me understand the power of the blessing even more. She said he had simply rolled back over in bed and started weeping before God. Why? See, shortly after I was born, my dad had left a very strong career in media as a news anchor that was only just beginning to climb the networks. He had left behind a potential lifestyle and financial security for our family to trust the Lord in ministry and in international missions. He worked all over the world while my mom joined him on her knees in prayer each step of the way. It was not always easy, to say the least, and unbeknownst to me, my dad had always feared that I would resent the life of ministry and faith they had said yes to. He feared that I would rebel and go the other way because of not having some of the extra luxuries that my friends might have, even though I always had far more than enough. But this is what makes the act of the blessing, rendering to me the release and freedom to go my own way with God, even that much more revolutionary. Usually, when we are afraid of something we try and hold onto it or control it. So, for my dad to struggle with that fear of me going the other way, yet still fully releasing me to God despite that fear, took more than most of us are willing to give. He empowered me in the face of his own fears, trusting me to God, and instead of that freedom being used to fulfill how he feared I would use it, he wept by seeing me come back even stronger and wanting to follow in his and my mom's footsteps, and see their ceiling become my floor.

A very similar dynamic played out with that original story my dad asked me to read in Genesis 27:1-40 about Isaac, Jacob and Esau. Now, many people know Jacob as the son who stole the birthright, and in a sense, that is true. But the details of the story reveal a couple things that are relevant to both the hope and battle for our kids' future.

Esau was the oldest son, and therefore, it was he who was in line to receive the father's blessing from Isaac. However, Esau had lost hope. He had lost vision for his life and seemed content to just survive the world that he was in. Jacob, though, was dying for purpose. He eagerly wanted to know his life meant something and was striving to get it. Both of those two things are true for our kids' generation as well. Their hearts are starved for purpose, and yet many have either lost hope for something more than survival or, sadly, perhaps they have never known anything, but surviving is even a possibility. That's where Esau was at. So much so that Esau basically told Jacob, "what need do I have for my birthright to be rendered to me, I just need something to fill me up for today." Like many of us do each day, which is easy in today's culture, Esau was willing to trade tomorrow's heritage for today's momentary needs. And when he realized how badly Jacob wanted the blessing, and likewise when Jacob realized he could capitalize on Esau's current state of perspective, they orchestrated a trade. Jacob didn't just steal the birthright, first, Esau gave it away for a bowl of stew. But that's not where the vital dynamics of the story stop, either.

The day finally came when Jacob had found a way to trick Isaac in giving him what Esau had already freely given away, but as the blessing from Isaac was being given, something jostled Esau's spirit that caused his perspective to wake up and realize what he was losing, as well as what he truly wanted in life. It says that after Isaac gave the blessing to Jacob, that Esau looked at Isaac and *"let out with a loud and bitter cry, Bless me, too, father."* That's the one that always gets me. Esau had the same innate cry that your kids have, that you and I both have; that cry from the core of our being to be valued, to be loved, to have purpose and to be believed in—according to who God created us to be. I believe that if you and I could walk around today with spiritual ears open, we would hear that same cry coming from people we pass by in all walks of life. Whether they are young or old, rich or poor, believer or not, all of us—everyone—has that innate desire within them and truth be told, most have not had someone to answer that cry the way my parents did for me.

Esau let out that cry while looking at Isaac, a man and therefore, a representation of the world. He was letting out the search for significance that had always been in him. And Isaac basically replied, "I'm sorry, but I don't have another blessing to give." I can't help but imagine the scene. I imagine Esau staring at his earthly father, begging to receive this blessing of value, worth and purpose for his life and heritage. Isaac can't answer it. But I imagine Esau's heavenly Father above him, ready to speak into his life, but Esau can't see or receive from God because he is still searching for man to fill that need for approval. See, that's the thing about the a "Father's Blessing" from a parent—it doesn't stop there! The blessing from a parent is powerful, but perhaps its greatest power is that it answers that internal cry we strive to fill up in so many ways that search for significance that for most people goes unfulfilled. When we receive that blessing from man, from an earthly parent or person of significance, it sets us free from striving for value or worth, from looking to fit in or for the approval of man and releases us to be able to look up and now receive directly from our heavenly Father who wants to give us even more!

How do I know? Because that's what happened with Jacob, and it is what happened for me as well. See, Jacob finally received what he longed for in that blessing from Isaac. It didn't answer all his needs in that moment, but it set him free to now begin his own path. And that path led him to what we famously know as Bethel, and Jacob's Ladder. That is the place where Jacob found rest from his striving, laying his head down on a rock. It is the place where God, as a heavenly Father, came to Jacob and gave him a similar blessing as to what Isaac had spoken, but now Jacob was getting the ultimate blessing straight from the Source. We can tell it was a surprising encounter for Jacob because he said, *"how awesome is this place... God was here the whole time, and I didn't even know it!"*

How often is that true? How often do we not even recognize the presence or blessing of God on our lives, for who He created us to be? We can't receive it because we are still so focused on getting from man or the world. But when we receive it from man the way Jacob did from his earthly father, Isaac, it sets us free to go forward in a way so that we can now receive the true blessing of identity and purpose straight from our heavenly Father. That is exactly what my father's blessing did for me, and it is what so many of our kids are longing for.

Jesus made it so that the blessing wasn't just something that was passed down from a father to their firstborn, whereas Isaac was found saying he didn't have another one to give. Through Jesus, we do! We have many more to give! We can take that heart of the father, and whether from a dad, from a mom, from a spiritual parent or mentor of some sort, we can impart the Father's heart of identity over our kids and their generation in a way that sets them free from striving for significance, so that they can start to receive their identity, their purpose and their light-shining marching orders directly from the Father Himself. We as parents have the charge to prepare this way for the next generation to receive the fullness of what God has always had for them, and all we must do is see through the Father's lens enough to render to our children what was always meant to be theirs.

As I mentioned before, that next year, after my own father's blessing, was full of powerful change and freedom to go forward in a renewed way. But I didn't know how important it was about to be as that year culminated just a few weeks before I turned seventeen. My dad was heading out on another one of his trips to Vietnam, working with the underground church as one of the primary nations he focused on. Just a few days before he left, my mom and another prayer partner and intercessor were coming over to pray over him before he left. That year I had started to join many of these prayer times, but that day I was at school. Until that is the loudspeaker went off in my second-period economics class. "Joey LeTourneau to the office to go home for a family emergency." Thankfully I knew the family emergency that day was joining the prayer time over my dad.

I'll never forget those moments sitting with him at the end of the prayer time, a son blessing his dad before his big trip, weeping together like brother and peer almost in the Lord. I was able to return a form of the blessing over my dad, appreciating him for who he was to me, to God, and to so many others. It was truly a God-orchestrated moment. And it was just three or four days later, while on his trip, that we received word that he had passed away while in Vietnam. Yet before this tragic loss that left such a hole, that year, my dad and mom had prepared the way for me to have that place filled directly by the Lord. I lost my dad just before turning seventeen, just eleven months after he gave me that father's blessing. But my heavenly Father was already so present in that place to comfort, to fill and to lead me forward as only He could do best. Before my dad went to his heavenly home all those years ago, he set me up to be fathered by God into all the plans and purposes that God had for my life. I miss my dad more than I can say, but he and my mom gave me everything by releasing me to the Lord in the way they did, it was the ultimate act of empowerment that has continued to live in my life and in our family heritage each day.

We've watched this same "Father's Blessing" give life, freedom, value and purpose to so many others around the world to this day. Street kids and orphans in Ethiopia, even adults here in the U.S., who never had a parent to give them such a thing as they were growing up. And we know God has plans to carry it to so many more across the nations in the days ahead. There are kids waiting on the other side of the world, and perhaps in your own home, who have that same innate cry to be valued, to be loved, to have purpose, and to be believed in. And it's you who are the missing link to give it to them. Who knows what will happen if you bridge that gap and render to your kids what the Father means for their life!

It can seem daunting to those who have never had someone offer such a blessing to them or to teach them how to give such a thing. But truly, your child just wants your heart to speak God's perspective of love, value and purpose over their life. There is no one way to format such a blessing, your children want to hear it from you in your own imperfect words. Your kids want to know that you see them, not just for what they are doing right, or doing wrong, but that you see them for who God truly created them to be on the inside, even if it is being covered up by the world. They want to know that there is a hope and future for their life, and they want to know they have your unconditional love and belief as they contend through the battle to walk in such a hope and future. Your kids need to know that your ceiling is their floor and that God made them unique on purpose because they are going to reach people that you never could have reached because they carry something that you don't have; and that's not only okay, but it's also a good thing.

You have the most privileged role in stewarding the value and light God put inside your children. I have no doubt you already know that. But we all need to be reminded sometimes—or even often. You have the power to give the next generation every chance to flourish in the hope and battle for their future. It's not politics. It's not school. It's not even church. It's you. You are that valuable and important in your child's life, not just to take good care of them and help them succeed, but to help them live out every bit of light God created them with, the very light you saw when you first laid eyes on them. The world needs to see that light, too.

WHERE TO START:

- Before you ever start to write a "Father's Blessing" for your child(ren), pray it first. Begin to till the ground of their heart in prayer first so they are ready to receive, and so that you are ready to give such.

- Render: Ask God what it is that He wants to give your child(ren). What is something unique to your child(ren) that the Father wants to remind them of, or for them to see about their life or purpose?

- Start to write out and prepare a Father's Blessing for your child(ren). Start with the oldest. Then pray about how and when you want to give it to them.

CALL TO ACTION:

"Where there is no vision, the people perish." (Proverbs 29:18)

This book has really been about giving you, as parents vision for what is possible in your kids, and through your kids, through God's eyes. There is a reason and a lot of truth, to why people perish when there is no vision. It is because the enemy has vision, and its actively set on taking ground inside our kids, inside our homes and families.

As we talked about, God has had a vision since the very beginning for building through family. And He works through that family to be fruitful and multiply, making disciples of all nations and taking ground in the world. It starts with our own families. It starts with our kids.

Are we going to pick up that vision? Are we going to allow the enemy to take ground in our kids and family, or is our family, our kids and their generation going to take ground in the world? There is no in-between. The enemy targets those waiting stagnantly in the in-between. We must have vision for our family. We have to help our kids find vision for their lives.

If we don't, who will? I don't want to find out.

But I can't wait to see a generation of our kids arise and shine in the world. I can't wait to see the creative genius and unique purpose that is primed to terrify the enemy in the world. I can't wait to see you as parent watch with joy as your kids become who God truly created them to be.

So, please don't wait. Start now.

 **END NOTES**

END NOTES

New Spirit Filled Life Bible. NKJV Edition
(Thomas Nelson Bibles, 2002)

Song: This Little Light of Mine. By Zilphia Horton and/or
Edward G. Ivins

George Land & Beth Jarman, Breakpoint & Beyond
(HarperBusiness, a division of Harper Collins Publishers, 1992)

Suzanne Collins. The Hunger Games. (Scholastic Press). 2008.

Wikipedia: Description and history of Purple

History of California Gold Rush - Website: Historichwy49.com

Forster, M. (2004). Finding Neverland. Miramax Films.

Seraph Creative is a collective of artists, writers, theologians & illustrators who desire to see the body of Christ grow into full maturity, walking in their inheritance as Sons of God on the Earth.

Sign up to our newsletter to know about future exciting releases.

Visit our website : www.seraphcreative.org

www.ingramcontent.com/pod-product-compliance
Lightning Source LLC
Chambersburg PA
CBHW051549120626
46551CB00013B/1436